Fleetwood Mac
THE DANCE

Project Manager: Carol Cuellar
Front and Back Cover Photography: David LaChapelle
Inside Photography (unless otherwise indicated): Neal Preston
Art Layout: Joseph Klucar

© 1998 WARNER BROS. PUBLICATIONS
All Rights Reserved

Any duplication, adaptation or arrangement of the compositions
contained in this collection requires the written consent of the Publisher.
No part of this book may be photocopied or reproduced in any way without permission.
Unauthorized uses are an infringement of the U.S. Copyright Act and are punishable by law.

Photo: David LaChapelle

CONTENTS

Photo: David LaChapelle

Big Love

Words and Music by
LINDSEY BUCKINGHAM

Medium Rock

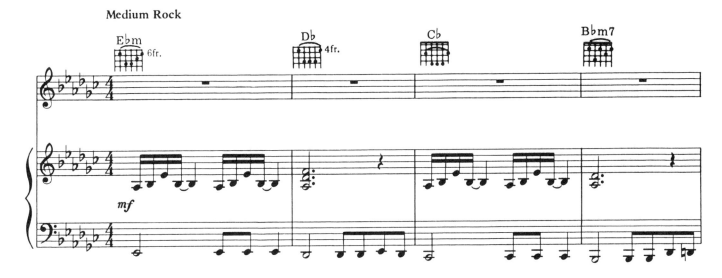

Look-ing out for love

Verse:

_____ me

3. (See additional lyrics)

in the night   so still.
and that   you al - ways will.

Big Love - 5 - 1
PF9742

© 1987 NOW SOUNDS MUSIC
All Rights Reserved

Oh, I'll build _____ you a king - dom _____ in that
Oh, you begged _____ me to keep you _____ in that

Chorus:

house _____ on the hill. _____ }
house _____ on the hill. _____ }
Look-ing out for love, _____

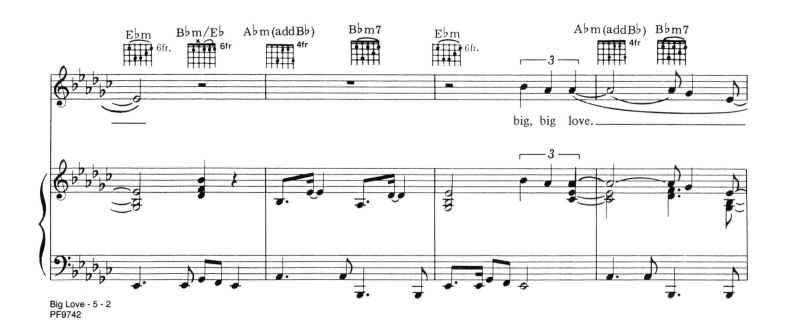

big, big love. _____

5

Verse 3:

I wake up
Alone with it all.
I wake up
But only to fall.

(To Chorus:)

Bleed To Love Her

Words and Music by
LINDSEY BUCKINGHAM

Moderate folk rock ♩ = 80

1. Once a-gain___ she steals___ a - way,___
2. Once a-gain___ she talks___ to me,___

then she reach - es out___ to kiss
then she van - ish - es in thin

Bleed To Love Her - 5 - 1
PF9742

© 1997 NOW SOUNDS MUSIC
All Rights Reserved

Verse 3:

The Chain

Moderately slow, with a beat

Words and Music by
LINDSEY BUCKINGHAM, CHRISTINE McVIE,
STEVIE NICKS, MICK FLEETWOOD and JOHN McVIE

© 1977 FLEETWOOD MAC MUSIC, NOW SOUNDS MUSIC & WELSH WITCH MUSIC
All Rights on behalf of WELSH WITCH MUSIC Administered by SONY/ATV MUSIC PUBLISHING,
8 Music Square West, Nashville, TN 37203
All Rights Reserved

Don't Stop

Words and Music by
CHRISTINE McVIE

© 1976 FLEETWOOD MAC MUSIC
All Rights Reserved

19

Don't Stop - 2 - 2
PF9742

Dreams

Words and Music by
STEVIE NICKS

Moderately, with a beat

Verse:

Now, here you go _____ a - gain._ You say you want_ your free -
Now, here I go _____ a - gain._ I see the crys - tal vi -

dom. Well, who am I _____ to keep_ you down?
sions. I keep my vi - sions to_ my - self.

Dreams - 5 - 1
PF9742

© 1977 WELSH WITCH MUSIC
All Rights Administered by SONY/ATV MUSIC PUBLISHING,
8 Music Square West, Nashville, TN 37203
All Rights Reserved   Used by Permission

24

Everywhere

Words and Music by
CHRISTINE McVIE

Medium Rock

Verse:

1. Can you hear me call - ing, out your name?_ You know_ that I'm fall - ing and I
2. Some-thing's hap-pen-ing, hap-pen-ing to me. My_ friends_ say I'm act - ing
3. *(See additional lyrics)*

don't know what to say._ I'll speak a lit-tle loud - er, I'll e - ven shout._
pe - cu - li - ar - ly._ Come _ on _ ba - by, we bet-ter make a start.

Everywhere - 5 - 1
PF9742

© 1986 FLEETWOOD MAC MUSIC
All Rights Reserved

'ry - where,___ I wan-na be with you ev - 'ry-where.

'ry - where.___ I wan-na be with you ev-

'ry-where.

D.S. %al Coda

Verse 3:

Can you hear me calling
Out your name?
You know that I'm falling
And I don't know what to say.
Come along baby
We better make a start.
You better make it soon
Before you break my heart.

(To Chorus:)

Say You Love Me

Words and Music by
CHRISTINE McVIE

© 1975 FLEETWOOD MAC MUSIC
All Rights Reserved

Lindsey Buckingham

Stevie Nicks

Mick Fleetwood

Christine McVie

John McVie

Landslide

Words and Music by
STEVIE NICKS

1. I took my love,_ I took it down._
2. See additional lyrics

Climbed a moun-tain and I turned a-round,_ and I saw_

Landslide - 5 - 1
PF9742

© 1975 WELSH WITCH MUSIC
All Rights Administered by SONY/ATV MUSIC PUBLISHING,
8 Music Square West, Nashville, TN 37203
All Rights Reserved   Used by Permission

D.S. % al Coda

I'm get-tin' old - er too._____ Oh,_____

Coda

a tempo

Well, the land - slide will bring it down._____

Oh,_____ the land - slide will bring it down.___

Verse 2:
Oh, take my love, take it down.
Climb a mountain and turn around.
If you see my reflection in the snow covered hills,
Well, the landslide will bring it down.
If you see my reflection in the snow covered hills,
Well, the landslide will bring it down.

Rhiannon

Words and Music by
STEVIE NICKS

Moderately, with a beat

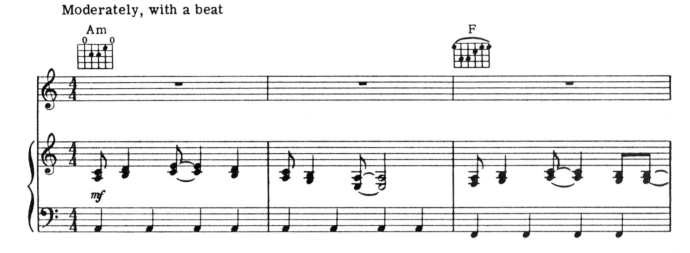

Rhi - an - non rings _ like a bell through the night. And
She is _ like a cat in the dark, and

would-n't you love _ to love _ her?
then she is _ the dark - ness.
Takes to the sky like a
She rules her life like a

Rhiannon - 4 - 1
PF9742

© 1975, 1977 WELSH WITCH MUSIC
All Rights Administered by SONY/ATV MUSIC PUBLISHING,
8 Music Square West, Nashville, TN 37203
All Rights Reserved   Used by Permission

My Little Demon

Words and Music by
LINDSEY BUCKINGHAM

Fast ♩ = 136

My Little Demon - 5 - 1
PF9742

© 1997 NOW SOUNDS MUSIC
All Rights Reserved

real-ly don't like it. I'm leav-in' it to you.

To Coda ⊕ 1.

2. My___

2.

Bridge:
F 5

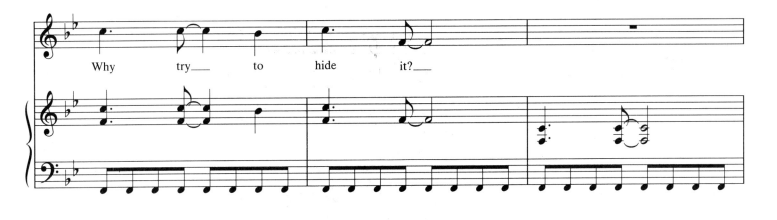

Why try___ to hide it?___

D.S. 𝄋 al Coda

Fight it.___   Fight it!___

Coda   N.C.

My lit - tle de - mon   is

com - in' af - ter me.   My lit - tle de - mon,

it's all____ that I can do to keep that lit-tle de-mon,

to keep that lit-tle de-mon, just to keep that lit-tle de-mon

a - way from you.

(Guitar solo till end)

1.2.3.

4.

I'm So Afraid

Words and Music by
LINDSEY BUCKINGHAM

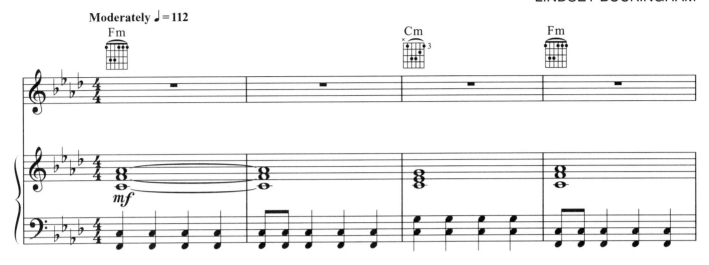

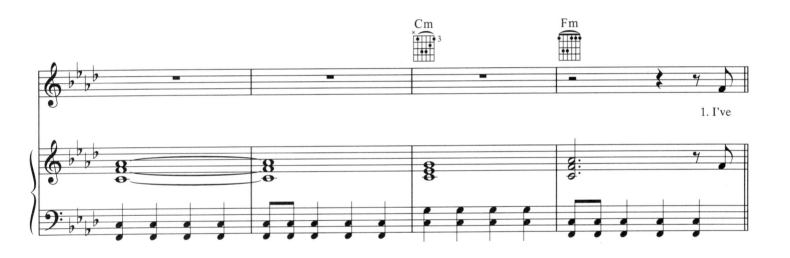

1. I've

been a-lone all the years. So man-y ways to count the tears.___ I
been a-lone, al-ways down. No one cares to stay a-round.___ I

© 1975 NOW SOUNDS MUSIC
All Rights Reserved

Go Your Own Way

Words and Music by
LINDSEY BUCKINGHAM

1. Lov-ing you is-n't the right thing to do.
2. Tell me why ev-'ry-thing turned a-round.

How can I ev-er change things that I feel?
Pack-ing up, shack-ing up is all you wan-na do.

If I could, may-be I'd give you my world.
If I could, ba-by, I'd give you my world.

Go Your Own Way - 2 - 1
PF9742

© 1976 NOW SOUNDS MUSIC
All Rights Reserved

Silver Springs

Words and Music by
STEVIE NICKS

Moderately slow ♩ = 84

1. You could be my sil - ver spring,_ blue - green,_ col - ors flash - ing.
2. *See additional lyrics*
3. *Instrumental solo ad lib....*

Silver Springs - 5 - 1
PF9742

© 1976 BARBARA NICKS MUSIC (Admin. by WIXEN MUSIC PUBLISHING, INC.)
All Rights Reserved   Used by Permission

Verse 2:
I begin not to love you.
Turn around, see me running.
I say I loved you years ago,
Tell myself you never loved me, no.
And if you say she was pretty,
And if you say that she loves you,
Baby, I don't wanna know.

Temporary One

Words and Music by
CHRISTINE McVIE and EDDY QUINTELA

1. Well, where are_ you, dar - ling, when_ my moon_ is_____ ris - ing and_ your

Temporary One - 5 - 1
PF9742

© 1997 FLEETWOOD MAC MUSIC and NEW ENVOY MUSIC
All Rights Reserved

the sea that di - vides___ us is a, a tem - po - rar - y one___

___ and___ a bridge will bring us back to - geth -

er?_____ Don't you know that ___

Verse 2:
What are you doing?
Going down into Soho once I get my rest tonight.
What are you doing?
Are you busy with your world?
Well, I wish you were busy with mine.
To Chorus:

Sweet Girl

Words and Music by
STEVIE NICKS

© 1997 WELSH WITCH MUSIC
All Rights Administered by SONY/ATV MUSIC PUBLISHING,
8 Music Square West, Nashville, TN 37203
All Rights Reserved   Used by Permission

Verse 4:
Still through the sunlight, days I wait.
Track, it goes through the fog.
Sun is burning me.
And you come running out in the wind with me.
The ocean is your blanket.
(To Chorus:)

Tusk

Words and Music by
LINDSEY BUCKINGHAM

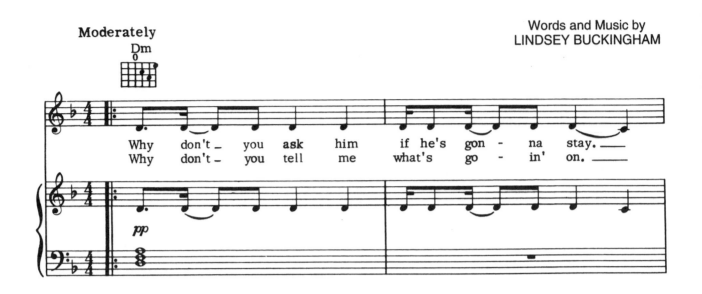

Why don't _ you **ask** him if he's gon - na stay. _
Why don't _ you tell me what's go - in' on. _

Why don't _ you ask him if he's go - in' a - way. _
Why don't _ you tell me who's on _ the phone. _

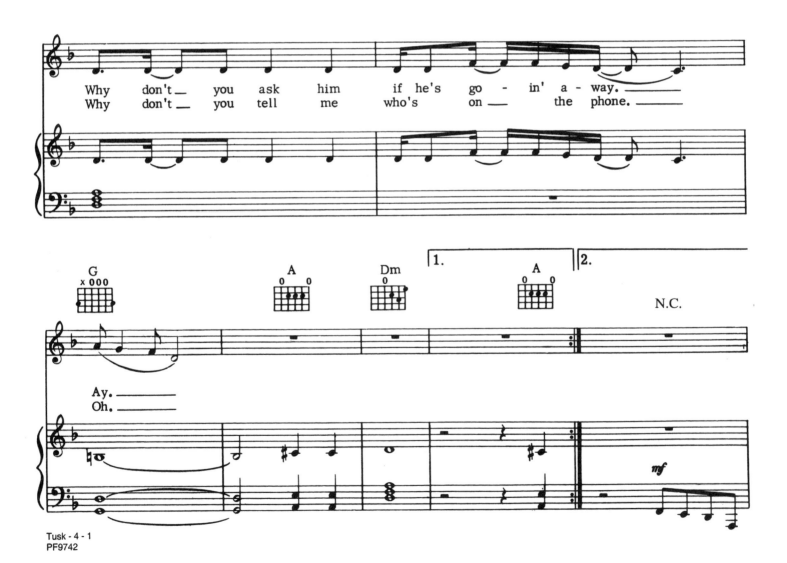

Ay. _
Oh. _

Tusk - 4 - 1
PF9742

© 1979 NOW SOUNDS MUSIC
All Rights Reserved

Why don't __ you ask him what's go - in' on. __

Why don't __ you ask him the lat -est on his throne. __ Oh, __

You Make Loving Fun

Words and Music by
CHRISTINE McVIE

1. Sweet,_____

2. *Instrumental*

© 1976 FLEETWOOD MAC MUSIC
All Rights Reserved

Photo: David LaChapelle

Fleetwood Mac